A KID'S LIFE IN
ANCIENT GREECE

SARAH MACHAJEWSKI

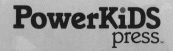

PowerKiDS press.

New York

Published in 2015 by The Rosen Publishing Group, Inc.
29 East 21st Street, New York, NY 10010

First Edition

Editor: Sarah Machajewski
Book Design: Michael J. Flynn

Photo Credits: Cover (artwork) © North Wind Picture Archives; cover, pp. 1, 3, 4, 6, 8, 10, 12, 14–18, 20, 22–24 (background texture) Ozerina Anna/Shutterstock.com; pp. 3, 4, 6, 8, 10, 12, 14–18, 20, 22–24 (paper texture) Paladin12/Shutterstock.com; p. 5 Peter Hermes Furian/Shutterstock.com; p. 7 Maria Grekos/Thinkstock.com; p. 9 http://commons.wikimedia.org/ wiki/File:Arte_greca,_pietra_tombale_di_donna_con_la_sua_assistente,_100_ac._circa.JPG; p. 11 (Parthenon) Nick Pavlakis/ Shutterstock.com; p. 11 (Athena) Dimitrios/Shutterstock.com; p. 13 DEA/G. DAGLI ORTI/De Agostini Picture Library/Getty Images; pp. 14, 20 Rogers Fund/The Metropolitan Museum of Art; p. 15 http://commons.wikimedia.org/wiki/File:Young_man_exomis_ Musei_Capitolini_MC892.jpg; p. 16 VOJTa Herout/Shutterstock.com; p. 17 Images Ect Ltd/Stockbyte/Getty Images; p. 19 http://en.wikipedia.org/wiki/File:Sanzio_01.jpg; p. 21 http://commons.wikimedia.org/wiki/File:Little_horse_on_wheels_ (Ancient_greek_child's_Toy).jpg; p. 22 f8grapher/Shutterstock.com.

Library of Congress Cataloging-in-Publication Data

Machajewski, Sarah.
 A kid's life in Ancient Greece / Sarah Machajewski.
    pages cm. — (How kids lived)
 Includes index.
 ISBN 978-1-4994-0025-0 (pbk.)
 ISBN 978-1-4994-0017-5 (6 pack)
 ISBN 978-1-4994-0018-2 (library binding)
 1. Greece—Social life and customs—Juvenile literature. 2. Children—Greece—Social life and customs—Juvenile literature. I. Title.
 DF77.M17 2015
 938—dc23
                             2014025939

Manufactured in the United States of America

CPSIA Compliance Information: Batch #CW15PK: For Further Information contact Rosen Publishing, New York, New York at 1-800-237-9932

CONTENTS

AN IMPORTANT CIVILIZATION

If you had to imagine what the earliest **civilizations** were like, what would you picture? You might picture cities, governments, and societies in which each person had a certain role. Ancient Greece had all these things. In fact, ancient Greece was so advanced that it's often called the "**birthplace** of western civilization."

Ancient Greece included all of present-day Greece, parts of present-day Italy and Turkey, and areas around the Aegean Sea. The civilization began around 3000 BC and lasted until 146 BC. Life in ancient Greece was unlike anywhere else in the world. Read on to learn more about it!

This is a map of modern-day Greece. Signs of the ancient civilization can still be seen in the country today.

AEGEAN SEA

GREECE

Athens

Sparta

MEDITERRANEAN SEA

5

ATHENS VS. SPARTA

Ancient Greece was not **united** as one country. It was separated into independent city-states. A city-state was made of a city and all the land around it. Each city-state had its own government, laws, and army. Athens and Sparta were two important city-states.

Life in Athens centered on education, art, and **philosophy**. People came to Athens from all over the world to study and trade goods. Sparta was a warlike state. Life there centered on training for battle and fighting wars. Demetria was an Athenian girl. Kyros was a Spartan boy. Their lives were very different.

Children played an important role in ancient Greece. They were raised to have skills that would help Greek society when they became adults.

GROWING UP IN GREECE

Though city-states were different, they had many things in common. Their people all spoke the same language, believed in the same gods, and shared the same **customs**.

CITIZENS OF ANCIENT GREECE

Demetria grew up in Athens with her father, mother, and brother. Demetria's father and brother were **citizens** of Athens. That meant they could vote to decide how to run the city-state. Women couldn't be citizens, so Demetria and her mother couldn't vote.

Kyros's family lived to take part in Sparta's warlike society. Men were soldiers. Boys trained to become soldiers starting at seven years old. Women and girls trained to be strong, too. Some Spartan men were citizens. Spartan women had great freedom and power, but they couldn't be citizens.

Slaves lived in both Athens and Sparta. Many of them were children. Some were born slaves. Sometimes families sold their children into slavery.

LIFE AND DEATH

Most Greek families were allowed to decide if they wanted to keep their children when they were born. However, in Sparta, the government decided. If babies were weak or sick, they could be left to die or become slaves.

GREEK GODS AND GODDESSES

Ancient Greeks believed gods and goddesses controlled every part of the world around them, such as the wind, water, and crops. They tried to keep the gods happy so their lives would be good. Greeks **worshipped** the gods at temples by making offerings to them.

Demetria's family often visited a temple called the Parthenon (PAHR-thuh-nahn). It was built in honor of the goddess Athena. She was very important to the people of Athens. The god Ares and the goddess Artemis were very important to the people of Sparta. Kyros and his family worshipped them at Spartan temples.

Each god and goddess stood for something. Athena was the goddess of wisdom. Ares was the god of war. Artemis was the goddess of the hunt.

ATHENA

PARTHENON

11

GREEK HOMES

Homes in ancient Greece were usually small. They were made of bricks and had a stone floor. The roof was covered with clay tiles. The windows had **shutters** to keep out the sun. Most homes were built around a courtyard, which is a small outdoor space in the center of a house.

Demetria's home in Athens was like Kyros's home in Sparta. Both homes had a courtyard and a farm. Demetria's entire family lived at home. Kyros and his father lived away in an army camp so they could always train for battle.

Many families used their courtyard as a place to practice their beliefs and pray to their gods.

13

TUNICS FOR ALL

Demetria and her mother made cloth. They used it to make clothes for their family. Demetria and her family wore the same kind of clothing other Greeks wore.

Ancient Greeks wore **tunics** called chitons (KY-tuhnz). Chitons came together at the shoulders and were belted at the waist. Women wore floor-length chitons, while girls, boys, and men wore chitons that ended at the knee. Old men often wore floor-length tunics.

Jewelry was popular in ancient Greece. This is an earring someone wore long ago.

Greeks wore a piece of cloth called a himation (hih-MAA-tee-ahn) around their shoulders. Himations were thin in the summer and thick in the winter. Many ancient Greeks wore sandals, but some went barefoot, too.

SPARTAN CLOTHING

The adults in Kyros's family wore chitons, just like Demetria's family in Athens. However, Spartan children didn't wear any clothes at all!

CHITON

THE GREEK DIET

Ancient Greeks ate olives, grapes, figs, and other fruits. They also ate eggs, fish, and bread. They didn't use forks or knives. They ate with their fingers!

Olives were the most important food in ancient Greece. The city-states were full of olive trees. Greeks crushed olives to make olive oil. They used the oil for cooking and to light their lamps.

GREEK OLIVES

Demetria's father was an important man in Athens. He often held dinner parties where men got together to discuss important topics. Demetria's brother was sometimes allowed to go to these parties. Demetria and her mother were not allowed to go.

IN THE KITCHEN

Girls like Demetria and their mothers were not allowed to eat in the dining room with the men. They ate together in the kitchen.

OLIVE GROVE

Spartans were too busy training to spend time growing food. Kyros's family had slaves, called helots, who grew all the food for his family.

A CLASSICAL EDUCATION

Education was a big part of life in Athens. Only boys went to school. Demetria's brother started school when he was seven. He studied reading, writing, music, and poetry. Boys also ran and wrestled to keep fit. Girls in Athens didn't go to school, so Demetria learned to read and write at home. She also learned how to cook, spin cloth, and do housework.

Kyros's education was all about becoming a soldier. He and other boys in the army learned how to read and write, but this wasn't as important as their fighting skills.

Athens was a center for learning. Many famous philosophers lived and studied there.

PAYING FOR SCHOOL

In ancient Greece, families paid teachers to teach their sons. Boys from poor families didn't get as much education as boys from rich families.

PLAYING GAMES

Kids in ancient Greece knew how to have fun! They played games that were much like the games kids play today. Spartan children like Kyros spent most of their time training. Sometimes they played games that showed their strength and fighting skills, since that's what they were good at.

Demetria played with dolls and tiny houses made of clay. Her brother wrestled with his friends. They also played with toys, such as tops, hoops, and balls. Greek children usually gave up playing with toys when they were 13 years old.

At 13, Greek boys and girls offered their toys to the gods. It was a sign of becoming an adult.

21

THROUGH THE YEARS

The ancient Greeks had many customs. Greeks, especially in Athens, spent a lot of time studying and thinking about life. They gave speeches in front of the whole city. They also acted out plays and wrote books that are still around today.

The ancient Greeks gave us something else important that's still around—the **Olympics**! Children were allowed to watch the events. Sometimes they even took part in them. Many customs from ancient Greece are still part of our lives, thanks to ancient Greeks such as Demetria, Kyros, and their families.

These ruins from ancient Greece help us imagine what life was like back then.

GLOSSARY

birthplace: Where someone was born, or where something began.

citizen: In ancient Greece, a person who had the right to take part in the business and government of the city-state.

civilization: A society with advanced ways of life.

custom: A traditional and widely accepted way of doing something that is specific to a society, place, or time.

jewelry: Pieces of plastic, metal, or other material you wear for decoration.

Olympics: A sports competition held every two years that began in ancient Greece.

philosophy: The study of knowledge and of right and wrong.

shutter: A moveable cover for a window.

tunic: A piece of clothing that covers the body from the shoulders to the knees or ankles.

united: Joined together.

worship: To pray to a god or practice one's beliefs.

INDEX

WEBSITES

Due to the changing nature of Internet links, PowerKids Press has developed
an online list of websites related to the subject of this book. This site is updated
regularly. Please use this link to access the list: www.powerkidslinks.com/hkl/gree